WHY CATS DO THAT

WHY CATS DO THAT

A COLLECTION OF CURIOUS KITTY QUIRKS

BY KAREN ANDERSON

ILLUSTRATED BY WENDY CHRISTENSEN

WILLOW CREEK PRESS®

Published by Willow Creek Press, Inc.
P.O. Box 147, Minocqua, Wisconsin 54548

Illustrations © Wendy Christensen
All photos © agefotostock.com except page 22 © Wildlife GmbH/www.kimballstock.com
and top of page 30 © Klein-Hubert/www.kimballstock.com

Printed in China

CONTENTS

PREFACE

Cats are like curious art objects come to life, and watching them go about their daily routine is sometimes like following around an art show. You're not sure what you'll see next, but you know it's going to be good. You plan on being captivated, entertained, enlightened, moved, astounded, possibly a bit disturbed and yes, even puzzled. These are some of the rewards of living with the enigmatic feline and this is the reason this book was written.

It is my belief that the cat is one of the most fascinating, graceful and beautiful creatures on the earth, and thus makes a wonderful subject to gaze upon and to study.

Part of the fun and challenge of being around cats is figuring out their sublime, even strange, ways of expressing things such as contentment, anxiety, affection, curiosity or anger. The fact that cats have retained so much of their wildness and so many of their strong, ancient feline instincts further invites long and loving observation. As with any animal, cats do peculiar things for their own reasons; the mystery that surrounds cats is particularly legendary.

Cat body language is covered in some detail here to take a bit of the guesswork out of determining your cat's true state of mind and heart; body language won't ever stop working and it cannot tell a lie.

A docile-looking cat may appear happy, but certain whisker, ear and tail positions might announce just the opposite. Wouldn't you like to discover what it all means? You can learn what your cat's body is revealing, and you'll be pleasantly surprised by the mutual enjoyment your efforts at deciphering will bring. It can only enrich the friendship you have with your cat.

Why Cats Do That is intended to embellish your general understanding of every domestic cat that treads the earth and to motivate you to thoroughly explore the beguiling ways of your own *felis catus*. Take the time to study, to photograph, to draw or paint these resplendent creatures. Indeed, may the cats in your life keep you quietly *oohing* and *aahing* for years to come.

WHY ARE CATS DEPRESSED WHEN WE LEAVE ON VACATION AND MAD WHEN WE RETURN?

We're not referring to boarding facilities here; the cat's disdain for spending time in a kennel was covered thoroughly in the previous section. Yet even if you've "seen the light"and allow kitty to remain at home with a cat sitter, don't expect her to receive any awards for being mature, understanding and polite about the whole thing. On the contrary, the cat will feel it's her duty to remind you how unthinkable it is for you to leave the premises longer than say, a day or two.

Cats have perfected this. They cannot quite believe we are leaving again, or at all, especially after last time. Kitty thinks, "They surely had to have noticed that I suffered greatly and barely recovered," or something along those lines. It is mystifying to the cat how we could venture out again, knowing their strong feelings about the issue. We can wish all we want that our intelligent feline grasps on some level the concept that we might need to get away, but it's not going to happen. The cat may also be wondering how we could so cheerfully leave—we become almost giddy about the adventure and the buildup is unbearable. Kitty begins to put two and two together and becomes unhinged at the thought of her impending doom and loneliness. Expect those piercing eyes to bore a hole right through you as it begins to dawn on the cat that you are in packing mode. She may gloomily hide for the better part of a day when she realizes she cannot change your mind.

I think the best possible scenario for cat care while you're away is to hire a good live-in cat sitter to stay with your feline family member(s). Cats are homebodies and contented loners if you compare them to dogs. Find a cat sitter who appreciates cats and finds them rewarding. Start contacting people early to procure the right person for the job. These people are out there and available; don't give up. Cats would rather stay in their home with their routines, surrounded by their scent, defending their kingdom *without* you rather than accompany you on vacation or get hauled off to a torture chamber, I mean boarding facility.

And then there's the homecoming. You've likely been counting down the hours until you get to see that amazing feline again, but kitty is clueless when you're going to return and any anticipation faded days ago. She is reservedly elated to see you and oh so relieved… but she's also miffed that you left at all and she'll likely let you know. It's like the mother who is reunited with her lost child—initially she's all hugs and tears, but that often switches to anger over the fact that the child wandered off in the first place. Kitty will be back to her normal self in a few hours. Or a few days. Or when she's good and ready.

WHY DO CATS LIKE CATNIP?

Well, there's just no sophisticated way to say this: cats like catnip because it gives them a "high." Catnip is really a drug for kitties. I'm not speaking of the same kind of drug habit that humans experience, though—catnip is generally considered quite safe. And it's not as if the cat frantically seeks out the catnip in order to achieve an altered state. If the catnip is around, then fine. If not, that seems to be all right, too.

There are two main theories as to how catnip affects cats; one is that it contains an odor similar to something in cat urine and the other is that the chemical nepetalactone, an unsaturated lactone found in catnip, acts as a drug.

Whichever it is, most cats usually take a brief drug trip from sniffing it, chewing it, and finally rolling in it—quite a frolicking frenzy to behold. Some say that prolonged indulgence may lead to personality changes in a small percentage of cats, but the vast majority of kitties are able to enjoy the 10 minutes of euphoria that catnip provides without any negative side effects.

WHY ARE CATS SUCH PICKY EATERS?

think cats have a stereotype to live up to. Advertisements portray cats as super finicky when it comes to mealtime and we've bought into the propaganda. If cat food manufacturers can convince us that cats are ultra-picky about their food, they've got us right where they want us because they've got the answer: their recipe in one hundred different flavors! How can we go wrong when there's so much variety to choose from and we're bombarded with the continual arrival of brand new, guaranteed-to-please concoctions?

Perhaps kitty is not naturally a fussy eater. Maybe kitty has become a fussy eater because we've fussed over her with one culinary treat after another. Does the offering of so many widely varying entrees actually condition the cat to expect change in her diet? What in the world have we turned kitty into… a nose-in-the-air foodie? Well sure, cats care about what lands in their food bowls and yes, they've got preferences like we all do, but I'm not sure they are quite so picky as we've been led to believe. They didn't start life that way.

Most kittens will hungrily chow down anything you put in front of them once weaned from their mother's underside. As cats grow and fine-tune their sense of taste they get curious about other kinds of cuisine and love to try new things. Store-bought cat treats are rarely refused. Finding the dog food is always great fun (but not recommended). The pantry floor is another good romp. And handouts from the toddler in the house… that can be a gold mine. A treat now and then is a good thing and won't disturb kitty's appetite as long as what she finds in her food bowl on a daily basis doesn't change much. Find a cat food your cat likes and generally stay with it. Rotate varieties on your schedule and kitty will learn that she gets what she gets! If she turns away from her regular food for a few days, don't worry and don't start parading new cat foods in front of her. When she's hungry, she'll eat. Be watchful though: a lack of appetite combined with lethargy or other symptoms means a trip to the vet to check for underlying problems.

WHY DO CATS LIKE MASSAGE?

Savvy and self-pampering, cats surely know a good thing when they see it—or feel it as the case may be. Massage is a form of therapy many humans have yet to experience but that shouldn't stop us from offering it to kitty. We all know that cats love to be petted at just the right time, for just so long and in just the proper places; the same applies to massage, or "deep petting." Cats like massage for the same reasons we like massage—it feels warm and wonderful. Massage relieves tension as muscle tissues are slowly worked and rubbed, allowing blood to flow freely and kitty to feel deliciously relaxed. Some of kitty's favorite places are the back of neck, chest, shoulders and down the spine. (Hint: start slow; proceed gently; stop if your cat gets the least bit unsure.) Kitty will likely begin purring and she may drop into a dreamy sleep, eternally grateful for your magical, soothing touch. Some cats devour long sessions of methodical all-over massage but most cats prefer a shorter time, perhaps 5–10 minutes. Kitty may gradually increase her appetite for massage as she becomes more comfortable with it. The trick, however, is getting her to return the favor to you—now that would be something to meow about.

WHY AREN'T CATS TRAINABLE?

A cat is not wired for training. Unlike dogs, cats don't possess the inner drive to obey their humans because cats do not have the inner desire to please their humans… simply for the sake of having a happy human around. It's more complicated than that. While canines can be trained to understand and perform, the feline can really only be trained to understand. The performing is entirely up to them. Cats wouldn't dream of being willing to be trained the way dogs are trained, but they are surprisingly eager to cooperate with some of our requests for the sake of our friendship. Determined and savvy, the feline is capable of learning to comprehend the meaning of countless words and phrases that pertain to our relationship with them.

But what about undoing some of kitty's misdeeds? Cats learn to modify behavior only by association. Kitty claws the back of the sofa; kitty gets water in its face from a spray bottle. Kitty nips at your hand, you blow a puff of air right into kitty's eyes. Once association has worked its disciplinary magic, your words alone will often be enough to correct your cat. Keep in mind though, kitty may not ever fully grasp why clawing the sofa or jumping onto the kitchen counter to sample the thawing meat brings such swift and troubling consequences.

When sharing life with a cat, it helps to remember that you're actually living with an animal that has become somewhat, but not fully, domesticated. Considering the cat's history as a solo act—a lone ranger, the extent to which this independent, self-managed animal cooperates with us is quite remarkable. I've long contended that cats desire our companionship and intentionally stay around to foster the relationship, all the while enduring our amusing, futile efforts to train and mold them to fit into our world view. And I happen to really like that about cats.

WHY DO CATS LIKE TO SLEEP ATOP US IN BED?

We are such lovable companions for our cats, and bedtime is a great opportunity for some heavy duty bonding with us! One look at a group of sleeping cats and you can see that they don't mind sleeping draped over one another, so why would we mind? It's just the feline custom to sleep in a group and cats are certainly not aware that humans may find it strange or annoying in any way. Our large, warm, uniquely-scented bodies offer security, coziness, and a whole heap of well-being for kitty, regardless of whether or not we share those particular sentiments. No matter—kitty will probably persist at lying on your head or your legs unless she eventually grows weary of getting tossed aside. Don't always be too quick to fling her away... she's your faithful feline friend and she just wants to stay close.

WHY DO CATS LOATHE THE WATER?

Rare is the cat that wholeheartedly enjoys spending time in water, but most cats don't mind the water quite as much as we think they do. They are intrigued by water and most like to play and flirt with water—on their own terms of course. (Think dripping faucets and shower drains.) Cats that live near water or descend from breeds that did, hence learned to fish, will happily dip a paw or two into a stream or lake if they think they can catch a fish or at least scare the poor fish enough to make it dart around. Since cats are natural swimmers—different than natural water lovers—it's not uncommon for a prowling feline to spot prey on the opposite side of a stream, dive in and paddle across to snag the tasty morsel. Only after a successful capture will the cat even stop to notice it got all wet in the process and start to lick that water clean off its coat.

This same cat however, will not likely relish a bath. Part of the reason is because it's never her idea. Aside from that, most cats just dislike being wet all over... and one explanation may be that water seems to interfere with the fur's ability to insulate the cat against the cold. However, if kitty becomes too curious for her own good and somehow gets into sticky, gunky things such as oil, grease, pitch, tar, etc. she will tolerate a lather-rinse-repeat bath, knowing it's the only way to restore her exceptional coat. (By the way, the reason cats don't need baths in the same way dogs need baths is because their tongues are like sandpaper and their saliva contains enzymes suited for breaking down the usual bits of debris that collect on the fur. Thus, cats spend an inordinate amount of time each day licking themselves clean from head to tail.)

Cats that genuinely love being in the water get lots of attention from onlookers; it's a thing to behold! With the exception of the Turkish Van cat breed, there's no predicting which cats will take to the water. 'Vans' originated near a particular lake in Turkey and for centuries have been famous for their love of the water. Now and then you'll see a regular Joe cat swimming around, just off somebody's rowboat or canoe, at the beach or even in a swimming pool. Often such cats began swimming lessons as kittens, with shallow water and their favorite kitty toys as bait. These cat owners are delighted with their aquatic cats and love to proudly show off their abilities as if to say, "See, cats adore the water!" Hmmm, cats who truly love the water are quite uncommon. And that's okay. Felines have more than enough going for them, don't you think?

WHY DON'T CATS COME WHEN THEY'RE CALLED?

Do you want the short answer or the long answer? The short answer: they don't want to come when they're called. The longer answer: they don't want to come when they're called because they really dislike being told what to do under any circumstance for any reason by any person at any time. This should remind you of the two or three-year-old in your life. Cats would rather be asked to do something with all of the politeness one can muster. A golden invitation is more their style. Seriously, when you open the back door and call your cat in for the night (good luck) it's much more effective to sweetly inquire of the cat if he wants to come inside rather than demand his return. No well-adjusted cat would respond favorably to a sharp beckoning and no self-respecting feline would cross the threshold of even the warmest house on the coldest night if he thought that punishment of any sort waited.

Cats are likely to come when they're called if they're motivated by what you've got for them.

For example, some cats will come running to the sound of a can of tuna being opened or the scrape of the cat's favorite brush against your hand. If kitty is in the mood for whatever you are suggesting he will waste no time materializing right before your eyes. It's not a good idea to falsely lure the cat though—he will remember that and you'll go backwards in the trust department.

With cats, sometimes you get the idea that you're supposed to feel very lucky if the cat returns at all. I mean, here is this slice of the wild that shows up back at the house time and time again, when it is perfectly suited to stay away and survive on its own. To acknowledge this is to begin to understand the capacity within cats for connection. The next time your cat comes when it's called, be thrilled. The next time your cat does not come when it's called, know that he's just out there being a marvelous specimen of cat. And you really wouldn't want it any other way, would you?

WHY DO CATS ALWAYS LAND ON THEIR FEET?

Well for starters, cats don't always land on their feet, but thankfully they make a safe landing nearly every time. After all, they only need 1.8 seconds to perfectly "right" themselves in the air and touch down with unbelievable grace, ease, and accuracy. In other words, even if a cat falls from a height of just one foot she technically has enough time and distance to accomplish this marvelous split-second maneuver. It all begins in the feline inner ear, where a signal is transmitted to the brain about the exact position of the cat's head in relation to the ground. Within nanoseconds, the brain orders the head to level itself and then the body follows by first twisting the upper part of the spine and then the rear half, so that at the right instant her entire body has been properly flipped into place. While all this is going on, the wondrous tail is rotating around acting as a very effective counterbalance.

WHY DO CATS SEEM SNOBBISH?

Few people would argue that many cats appear snooty as they roam throughout their day. Here comes the feline with that slow, important strut, those measured tail movements, head held high and a casual, regal glance or penetrating stare. Even their playfulness can seem a bit tempered. While the feline has much to feel superior about, I don't think it necessarily looks down upon those it considers somewhat inferior, which is the attitude of a true snob. And if cats were the unbearable elitists some think they are, they definitely wouldn't make such a habit of seeking the company of us lowly types. So why does the feline act like we and the rest of the animal kingdom are entirely beneath it? How can the steely eyes of a singular cat manage to deconstruct our ego? Do they practice this look? Do they even give a rip?

Okay, let's unravel some of this. I would have to agree that the feline seems to look down his aristocratic nose at just about anything that moves, but I don't think they dislike us. Not at all. Nor do I believe they are merely tolerating our ways. I'm convinced we humor them endlessly and I think they are often puzzled by how humans behave (and other animals who share their world). Infinitely curious about our strange customs, cats are keen observers with lots of time to study us—and in their estimation we must be quite a piece of work. To them we are, for starters, an odd species of hairless hind leg walkers who rarely sit still, appear ignorant about the benefits of relaxation, don't have a clue how to hunt and seem to have forgotten that we are actually nocturnal! Kitty conjures up all kinds of theories in an attempt to make sense of humans. Perhaps kitty is not so much feeling high & mighty as downright confused and even the slightest bit sorry for us. In their minds, maybe we have much to learn… and too little hope of learning it. Maybe they're sticking around in part, to teach us. And that's not snobbery.

WHY DO CATS FIGHT WITH EACH OTHER?

Cats are autonomous, territorial animals by nature. In the wild, felines live in very small families or alone, with little need to interact outside these compatible groups to survive. Unlike the dog, who operates with a pack mentality—"how are *we* going to solve this problem… how are *we* going to find our next meal… defend ourselves… find a lost pack member," etc. Cats think mostly about themselves. It's not selfishness, it's self-sufficiency. This self-governing trait leads to a severe lack of effective skills to solve disputes. Domesticated cats function much the same way; they usually do not hang out with each other amicably unless they've been raised together from kitten hood. What we typically see from the local feline community is a tenuous tolerance towards one another and cats have perfected this stance. Weeks can pass with no sign of catfights and you might erroneously believe there is harmony in the cat world, but it's probably the calm before the storm. Inevitably problems arise when other cats in the neighborhood do not respect well-marked territorial boundaries. And because cats are cats, the territorial boundaries are frequently not respected.

Cats are simply not able to stay within their own territory. A powerful survival instinct drives them to increase their kingdom even if it means overthrowing the ruling regime in the land. At the core of this compulsion is the desire to have ample private hunting grounds. Cats continually chase each other out of their territories, jockey for position and carefully track the others' flagrant missteps. This is serious business for cats and if you've ever witnessed a catfight you know what I'm talking about. When a trespassing cat has crossed the line one time too many and refuses to heed warning after warning, the whole feline population hears about it—and we do too. The unearthly cries of an incensed feline are loud and bone chilling, disturbing the deepest of human sleep. At this point in the contest the cats are fully engaged and ready to rip mercilessly into one another. If one cat decides to back down the fight de-escalates and they may take issue again some other night. If nobody retreats it's war and oh my, watch for flying fur.

Somehow the cats figure out who won and the boundaries are once again negotiated. It's ancient and fascinating and quite unsettling for the rest of us, but the cats themselves seem pleased that something critical got resolved and perhaps even all-out disaster averted. I certainly hope so—that's a whole lot of claws, teeth and energy expended for just a drill. But brace yourself, the intense feline battles are not likely over for good—cat relationships are notoriously fragile and the majority of cats do live with a fair amount of tension between them. Oh the drama.

WHY DO CATS ARCH THEIR BACKS?

A cat with an arched back is in a fearful, defensive mode and he's trying to make himself look larger and more threatening. Cats are able to arch their backs so high because their spines contain nearly 60 vertebrae, twice what we have. They demonstrate this incredible flexibility when trying to intimidate each other. Often kitty will turn sideways to display an even more impressive profile, or his coat will fluff up as well, thus the descriptive phrase, "its hair was standing up on end." This adds to the heightened and fearsome look. What's happening is that certain hairs are responding to an adrenaline rush. When kitty feels superior, it's just the hair along the spine that sticks up. If kitty perceives he may not be in the stronger position during an encounter, his entire coat may stand up. These are great looks for cartoons, but probably not what we want to see very often from our own little darlin's.

WHY DO CATS DISLIKE RIDING IN A CAR?

There is absolutely nothing about this experience that cats even remotely think is okay. It helps to imagine how much dogs love to ride in the car and then realize that for cats it's the antithesis of this emotion. For one thing, you're immediately and dramatically taking them out of their beloved territory and that is never a good idea. To a cat, it is akin to leaving the fort unprotected and the kingdom in peril. That alone is nerve-wracking and kitty is unbelievably stressed. (Okay, so you know of a cat that enjoys riding in a car? I'm referring to the other 98%.)

Unlike dogs, who typically find going anywhere by any means for any reason with their human friend and master a complete and total joy, cats would rather stay home, thank you very much, and guard the property. For dogs and their people, going on a walk or driving around in the car is a fun, bonding activity that brings great waves of well-being and security. Just the opposite happens with kitty. She feels disconnected, vulnerable and very possibly terrified. Nothing is predictable. Everything that is familiar and safe has vanished. Gone are her home, her neighborhood, her scent markings, her whole world and she has no reason to believe she will ever return.

A sturdy cat carrier is essential when transporting a cat anywhere. It might seem odd, but kitty is more secure in the confines and privacy of a small carrier and can find some solace tucked in there with her own blanket. If a cat gets the run of the car it might squish under a seat or wander anxiously—either way the cat is at much greater risk if there's a collision. Some cats sit in angry or frightened silence while others meow non-stop. Kitty is not pleased and you will likely hear about it, despite efforts on your part to alleviate her fears. This uprooting is not okay with cats and the sooner the nightmare ends the better.

It's too bad that vets don't make house calls. Cats would surely appreciate that. Since most cats abhor car rides, their owners only take them in the car to visit the vet, which of course reinforces the notion that the harrowing car trip always concludes at the same horrendous destination: the dreaded vet. To a cat, the vet is a completely unnerving place with 10,000 different dizzying cat scents, the presence of dogs for pete's sake, no place to hide and worst of all, no way to escape. Enduring the actual exam and, heaven forbid, the lab work is all kitty can do until the return trip home. Oh, and it's best not to take the long, scenic route on the way back to try and condition the feline that car riding is any kind of fun adventure. C'mon, you know you were thinking about that.

WHY DO CATS TORTURE THEIR PREY?

Granted, it seems so cruel of kitty to slowly kill the hapless mouse, shrew, bird, bug or whatever it is she's nabbed. But the truth is, cats aren't intentionally mean and nasty. It's commonly thought that cats are purely having fun with their latest catch by prolonging the hunting game and thus, the poor critter's life. Kitty isn't aware that she is torturing the tasty, moving morsel and she certainly won't be able to comprehend your explanation nor understand your reprimand if you attempt one. Cats will do what cats will do!

Some cat experts have actually stated that they wonder if a well-fed cat (who doesn't hunt out of necessity) is even all that sure of what to do with a mouse once it's caught, so they just sit there and toy with it! However, since much of the cat's behavior is instinctive, I don't happen to agree.

Here is a thoughtful alternate possibility of what might be going on: since cats do not torture their prey every single time, could it be that the feline has flickers of mercy towards the very animal she is contemplating for her next meal? Could the cat actually be giving its prey one last fighting chance? I admit, this is a view only a true cat lover could ponder.

(Please note: The songbird population is drastically affected by house cats; as a conscientious cat owner, it may be best to leave kitty inside or tethered to a short leash.)

WHY DO CATS MEOW?

It's not a growl or a bark or a roar. It's not a squawk or a tweet. And it's surely not a honk or a quack! A meow is the cats melodic, passionate song of deep feeling and expression. It is poetry and it is enchanting. Defining and describing the many meows seems impossible. There are people who study cat vocal utterances very seriously and claim that they can understand much of what cats are trying to say. Consider some gleanings from the vast world of cat meows most often heard from the domestic feline. As you listen intently to your cat, you'll be charmed at the kaleidoscope of distinctive sounds. Here are a few to get you going:

"HELLO"

The tone in kitty's voice is upbeat, friendly, and hints of anticipation. This is a shorter meow, and often is accompanied by a loving rub or hop onto your lap. Cats use this when entering a room or greeting you at the door.

"I WANT SOMETHING"

This meow is more like a whine and ranges in intensity from very mild to downright grating. Cats love to perfect this—they try to wear us down and make us give in! This meow is used by a lonely or hungry cat, a cat who smells raw meat, a cat who is desperately trying to lure you to play, or anytime kitty really wants something! Note where kitty is and what she might be wanting. Some cats will walk towards the desired thing if encouraged by a willing human.

"IS IT OKAY TO... ?"

Kitty almost sounds like she's asking a question when she uses this meow; in fact that's usually just what she's doing. It's a soft, vibrating utterance that is so endearing you cannot possibly say "no" to whatever it is! Cats avail themselves of this meow when they are in a certain mellow mood and wish for a blessing for something they'd like to do. It could be a desire to come up onto your lap, to be finger fed a dot of yogurt, or to be allowed into a particular nook that's normally inaccessible. This is not a demanding meow and that could be why it's so hard to turn down.

"GET CLOSER AND I'LL MAKE YOU WISH YOU DIDN'T"

Watch out for this one. It doesn't even sound nice. Kitty is unhappy with whatever it is you're doing to him or with him. This meow is more like a low-pitched war cry that is meant to warn or suffer the consequences! It can be short, or long and drawn out. Cats battling over territory will use this on each other.

WHY DO CATS ROAM AT NIGHT?

Of course part of the answer to most every cat behavior question that ends with "at night" is this: because they are nocturnal. In other words, cats are naturally more active and wakeful at night and prefer to slow down and sleep during the day. (Domesticated cats adapt somewhat to our peculiar awake-during-the-day routine, especially those which are warmly and habitually integrated into our lives and schedules.) In the world of the cat, nighttime is the time for getting some business accomplished. When the sun goes down the tail goes confidently up and the cat is primed for stepping out and living large. Let the night rituals begin!

Anytime from dusk to dawn cats might be out wandering, but not without a mission. Far from roaming aimlessly, kitty has some real work to do. Assuming the cat receives regular meals, his first priority outside at night is not hunting, which would be the case for cats in the wild or feral cats. Nothing beats a good mouse chase and even if kitty is not hungry, it's hard to resist a game of "How fast can I catch the tender little varmint?". Probably the next item on the to-do list is patrolling their territory and this can consume a bit of time, depending upon how many blocks or acres the cat has claimed. Along with making a visual security check at various spots along the way, the feline must mark and re-mark fences, signs, posts, steps and trees with its special scent gland secretions that serve to remind other cats this is private property.

Besides all that, cats attend to miscellaneous feline community issues at night; well, not only at night but also at night. More cats are likely to be roving around after dark and it's a grand opportunity to socialize. Kitty might hang with a feline buddy and just watch stuff, confront some unpleasantness that requires attention, or grab a friend and go terrorize a dog. And in case you're wondering, darkness doesn't hinder cats' after-dark activities in the least. A cat's eye, designed with a unique, reflective lining at the back of the eye and greater dilation in low light, are suited for night vision. You've no doubt been taken aback at the eerie reddish or greenish glow in a cat's eyes when there's very little light present. That's what I call "special effects."

WHY DO CATS SCRATCH THE FURNITURE?

Cats view our furniture as truly the most divine scratching apparatus that could be conceived of, and they must be entirely confused when we dissuade them from using it for the obvious intended purpose! There sits the wicker love seat, the upholstered chair and that nice big sofa, just waiting for kitty to sharpen her claws at whim.

Actually, cats aren't technically sharpening their claws as they scratch, but are instead stripping away the old, dull claw sheaths to expose brand new sharp claws beneath. This is a powerful feline instinct that drives the cat to keep its claws in top form at all times. While kitty is vigorously scratching, her claws are also getting practice extending and retracting, which is essential to catching prey, fighting and climbing. The front legs and shoulders are getting stretched and strengthened too, depending on how fervently the cat is scratching.

And don't forget the ever-important scent marking! There are scent glands on the underside of the front paws which are madly secreting kitty's special mark.

Scratching can also be deployed as an attention-getting tool, simply because the cat has figured out that the sound of shredding furniture can easily get you to notice her. But don't dismay—with some gentle, consistent correction and the presence of a large, sturdy scratching post, you can probably save most of your furniture.

WHY DO CATS NIBBLE ON HOUSEPLANTS?

Most cats that eat the leaves of house-plants aren't able to get outside and chew on outdoor plants. Cats are primarily carnivorous, but they love to sample vegetation now and then. For indoor-only cats, you get to stay one step ahead of kitty and provide her the proper plant munchables to satisfy the yearning, instead of leaving it up to feline whim. Since grass contains a beneficial B vitamin (folic acid) that felines need and there-fore seem to crave, little grass seedling packs are the way to go indoors. Catnip seedling sets are available as well. Both are easy to grow and kitty will be ever so thankful.

Another reason cats like to eat plant leaves or grass is to aid in digestion (calm their upset tummy) or to force the upchucking of a nasty hairball. When the most unpleasant sensation comes over them to eject the annoying ball of ingested fur, sometimes it just helps to eat some-thing that they know will make them vomit. Pretty smart, really.

And no discussion of cats eating plants would be complete without mentioning plant material that is poisonous to cats. The list is surprisingly long and it contains some very common culprits such as ivy, azalea, rhododendron, tomato and beans. There's a bunch of tropical plants (indoor in most parts) also known to be toxic to cats. This is how I weigh in on this sobering information: it is correct that specific plants could cause illness or even death to a feline, but I don't entirely omit these plants from my house or garden. However, I do avoid over-using these plants and I take care to provide my cats with plenty of safe things they love to eat, like catnip and catmint. It's a risk, but a calculated risk that I manage and monitor reg-ularly. The percentage of cats that eat enough poisonous plant material to get sick is low. Act wisely and reasonably within your comfort zone and hope and pray for the best.

Keep in mind too, that sometimes a miserably bored and under-stimulated cat will start to nibble on plants. Cats should be related to, entertained and involved in your day to day life. Beyond that, rearrange the houseplants to mix things around a bit and pick up some designated cat greens the next time you're at the market.

WHY DO CATS SEEM SO ALOOF?

Most standoffish cats didn't start out that way. Somewhere along the line, cats like this were repeatedly mishandled, excluded, ignored or frightened by humans who just didn't understand the feline psyche. Often accused of being haughty, cold and disdainful, the cat has really had to work diligently at shaking this poor reputation. Cats are sensitive, responsive creatures who usually require humans to take the initiative when it comes to affection and involvement.

Of course, there are exceptions, but generally speaking, the cat looks to us to set the household standard for closeness and "together time." If we don't go out of our way to deliberately invite kitty into our everyday lives, kitty will keep her distance. If we don't bother to shower kitty with affection, she will reciprocate. And so on (I think you get the idea). But here's the good news: once a cat is heartily welcomed into the family, you are granted the privilege of watching her blossom and develop into a tender, loving feline! Of course, cats aren't going to respond with the same effervescence and energy of dogs, but within the context of feline expression, it's safe to predict that you will be thoroughly charmed and thrilled by your cat's warm acceptance of you and her sincere desire to be in your midst. Given the opportunity, most cats will gladly come close—and the word "aloof" slips entirely from one's vocabulary.

WHY CAN'T CATS MAKE UP THEIR MINDS WHETHER TO BE INSIDE OR OUTSIDE?

The answer is simple but the solution is impractical and problematic. Cats possess a primeval instinct to gain access to their entire territory at absolutely all times of the day and night. Regardless of how seldom this occurs, the feline urge to roam freely and frequently through their hard-fought territory is firmly entrenched in their DNA. From the feline point of view, unrestricted admittance to their portion of the world outside the door is a given and the cat is certain its survival, security and reputation are at stake. Scent marking (and re-marking) every corner of the terrain is uppermost in a cat's mind when that maddening door finally opens. A cat employs its powerful scent glands on every single trip outside your house, whether you realize it or not. Equipped with pheromones, a chemical totally unique to each cat, the glands secrete this potent scent on command and the cat deposits it to announce all kinds of things like, "This is my property," "I was here" or even "I am looking for a mate." These nifty glands are found on the cat's cheeks, along the tail, under the chin, on the lips, around the ears and even between the toes. Kitty can hardly avoid scent marking if she moves at all—a fact she knows well and makes use of incessantly and to her advantage.

How often does your cat ask to go outside by way of a verbal utterance or that unmoving, high alert presence at the door, only to step outside briefly and then meow to come back inside? You know what often happens next: kitty is inside for a bit and before you've had a chance to make a pot of tea she changes her mind and demands to be let out once again. This drama repeats itself more often than we'd care to admit—and while we are tromping over to the door for the very last time (yeah, right) we ask the cat why it cannot seem to make up its mind. I wonder if kitty is not so much indecisive as she is stressed that she must choose either inside or outside and is forced to ask unless the door happens to be open. It's not as if she scoots outside and then remembers she really wanted to go sit in the window sill. What the cat truly desires is the (okay, I'll say it) luxury of traveling back and forth with ease to perform the ongoing and necessary tasks that all cats naturally do.

Installing a cat door is often the ideal solution, and it does work beautifully, if the other cats in the area do not feel it their right to use the same cat door to enter our homes. For some cats in some households in some neighborhoods, cat doors are the answer and those of us who don't live in that kind of environment are envious, to be sure. Until then, keep letting down that drawbridge for your royal highness.

WHY ARE CATS SO PERSISTENT?

'm particularly fond of this feline character trait as it points to the cat's indomitable optimism. Perhaps optimism is not a quality most folks readily see in cats at first or even second glance, but I'd contend that the feline is indeed a stalwart optimist, albeit with a generous dose of pensive melancholy added to the mix. As cats meander through life they seem to have adopted a cheerful attitude of, "It sure can't hurt to ask!" when something irresistible grabs their attention or they merely wish to state their desires.

The cat's assertiveness and tenacity over matters they're passionate about is a curious, wonderful thing and though admirable, sometimes absurd to those of us in attendance. Whether a feline is pleading once again for the halibut that has been cooked to perfection yet sadly never makes it into his mouth, or purring loudly on your chest every morning at an hour you're never, ever vertical, it's like it never occurs to the cat that our one-hundredth answer will be the very same as our last ninety-nine answers. What is going on here? Is kitty that dense? How does the saying go… the definition of insanity is doing the same thing over and over and expecting different results? We surely cannot be talking about the enlightened feline here.

As sure as the sun comes up, various commentators will reason that this feline-pushy persistence is not indicative of smarts or anything else positive, but instead a sign of lesser intelligence, bordering on questionable mental health. Nothing could be further from the truth. There's an enduring hopefulness about cats that has served it well over the centuries. Cats have thrived in conditions that would zap the confidence right out of many an animal, but the feline hangs in there with quiet gusto. They have a knack for anticipating the best but preparing for the worst and that's not a bad methodology. Far from how our wide-eyed, tail wagging, head tilting dog companions display their forever hopeful spirits, our cats can look almost stoically hopeful. "You just never know," the cat seems to muse, "the unexpected does happen and therefore I'll opt for having hope." So that's sheer optimism you're sensing when your cat appears oblivious to what's been in place for years in your household—he simply refuses to give in, ahem, I mean give *up*. And I'll proudly take that kind of guy on my team any day.

WHY DO CATS MAKE A FUNNY CHATTERING SOUND?

This has got to be the weirdest sound to arise from kitty. It's an oddly charming sound that cats produce when they see prey that cannot be reached because of some obstacle in the way.

You may notice this "chirp" when your cat is looking out from a favorite window at the backyard birds, wishing he could get to them. The cat opens its mouth slightly, pulls its lips back, and then opens and closes its jaws very rapidly. The noise that results is a cross between what we know of as lip smacking and teeth chattering. If kitty is going extra wild with excitement, she might add a curious vocal utterance almost like a cry that really makes the whole thing sound peculiar!

The cat isn't attempting communication, she's just frustrated that she cannot catch this critter and inflict her legendary "killing bite." She sits there and practices the skilled move instead, relegated to merely dreaming of the snack that might have been.

WHY DO CATS STARE AT THEIR NEW TOY WITH PUZZLEMENT?

The most accurate answer is this: because you didn't bring home a live mouse! Your cat is waiting for the day a real critter arrives home in that pet store bag and until it does, you're going to have to make the fake one do something mighty interesting. Cats won't saunter over, grab a toy and bring it to you like a dog. Stir up some pretend play and make the object seem ALIVE. That is the magic to all things about cats and play: it's got to be hunting practice or it isn't play—it's just an activity without a purpose or a point. For example, the cat toy consisting of a dowel with feathers tied on the end must dip and dart and hide for a few seconds under something before it moves again, to mimic the movements of a feathered or furry thing trying to escape the cat.

Oh, how we love to buy cat toys. We find a clever new one and wonder if we've finally discovered the toy that will engage our cat until the end of time. It's splendid in the beginning and we play with our cat for a while, but soon grow weary of the whole thing. Store bought cat toys are great if they get used. You can't go wrong with the fuzzy little mice. This tried-and-true mouse with the suede tail is available everywhere and can

hardly be beat. Throw it up a flight of carpeted stairs and watch kitty chase it, flip it up and then go after it. If you do this enough times with her she may eventually play this on her own, but you do need to interact now and then to keep it going. Don't forget to look around the house and create some toys with what you've already got. Small balls of aluminum foil work nicely. Fill a sock with freshly dried catnip and knot it... kitty will be full of glee and goofiness, plus it's easy and affordable. Stray Lego pieces or large buttons can get lots of mileage on hardwood or tile floors.

Involve the scratching post and climbing gyms that adorn your house as well; dangle things around the various levels and watch kitty invent hunting games with flair and strategy. The cat will find things to amuse herself if you neglect to play with her and provide appropriate items and you might not appreciate her choices. Favorite times of the day are at night when you are about to fall asleep of course. But that's only because she's been under-exercised all day and this is her last chance to lure you into some merriment. You'll know that you've been on the right track with play time when you bring home a toy and the cat actually shows some excitement.

WHY DO CATS' EYES CHANGE SO MUCH?

We may not always be able to determine what a cat is saying with his eyes, but we can see that a cat's eyes are ever-changing. The cat's awesome, expressive eyes are discussed here not in an attempt to positively decode them, but to playfully enjoy and explore them. This dimension of your cat's body language is highly subjective and open to all kinds of entertaining interpretation. The following descriptions are meant to prompt your own ponderings about your cat's eyes.

WIDE OPEN EYES

Alert? intense? interested? terrified? surprised? anxious? excited? unsure? bewildered? shocked? anticipating?

HALF CLOSED EYES

Studying? surveying? solving? wondering? relaxed? sleepy? content? bored? pretending to be bored? suspicious?

EYES ARE JUST SHOWING A SLIVER

Really relaxed? really sleepy? really borded? really suspicious?

EYES ARE OPEN BUT REPEATEDLY CLOSING HALF WAY

Adoring? wishing? hoping? yearning? imagining? pleading? placating? longing?

WHY DO CATS LIKE TO HEAR US TALK?

Because silence is not always golden. Cats have more or less chosen to dwell among us in our modern society and as our relationship with them develops, they hear us talking with other family members and want to be included. Our words are (hopefully) mostly pleasant, and perhaps even lilting, and kitty finds it lovely and interesting and comforting. Conversations ebb and flow in their midst and while they cannot decipher all that we say, they do comprehend the tone and earnestness. Kitty becomes drawn in… even if he doesn't always let on.

If you see your cat perched somewhere or hanging over the edge of a table or ledge looking at you in a coy, placating sort of way, it could be longing for you to mosey over and say a few words. It's a certainty if the cat responds with various little meows and a slight turn of the head as if to say, "I'm here too and I could use some dialogue, people." Understandably, cats have earned the reputation for being rather low maintenance and while that is true to a minimal degree, the reverse is also true—the cats in our lives need much more involvement and chit chat that we ever give them credit for. Okay, so we're not talking about anything hard or complicated here. Besides a few intentional greetings and inquiries over the course of your day, just banter on while you're doing other tasks. Use the cat's name often and affirm all the awesome feline things he does throughout the day. Announce to him when you're going out and tell him that he was missed when you return. Don't assume that your cat could care less if you speak with him or not! Treat kitty like a valued member of the family and he will begin to regard you differently too.

You need not and should not attempt to sit down with kitty and say, "Here's your quality kitty time for the day… so let's be efficient about this and talk!" Good heavens the cat will see right through that performance and you won't be any farther along. Instead look for brief, authentic moments of tender, one-to-one verbal exchanges and you might be surprised how the cat thrives under that level of connection. Go ahead, converse with that cat of yours; you know you want to. Make the first move and see what happens. Nobody is listening… except your cat.

WHY DO CATS MAKE THAT STRANGE GRIMACE?

Cats sometimes do a funny thing with their mouths when they come across a delightfully complex smell. Technically known as the "flehmen response," it is a feline reaction to an exceptionally enjoyable scent. The cat is usually walking along and maybe sniffing at this and that, only to stop abruptly. The cat will lift his head slightly, ease back his upper lip, and then open his mouth just a little. Kitty holds this position for a few seconds—mesmerized and intoxicated by the smell. The opened mouth allows the special fragrance to pass through and be studied and enjoyed by what's called the Jacobsen's organ, located in the roof of the cat's mouth. It's really a smell-taste organ about 1/2 inch long that cats use to analyze intriguing smells in and around their territories. This must be a pleasurable activity for cats, as they are completely lost in thought and entirely captivated by the encounter. It's an experience we humans cannot enjoy and must only guess at. Could it be something like the combination of smelling a heady flower and tasting a fine wine or a multi-layered French sauce at the same time? Who knows? But it does make me a little envious of the cat.

WHY DO CATS CHASE BIRDS?

cannot readily think of another subject that pulls at the hearts (and consciences) of people with cats quite like this topic. Cats who are allowed to wander outside in our densely populated, bird-habitat-challenged neighborhoods are the subject of hot debates involving their right to hunt versus the birds' right to live. The chasing, teasing and ultimate capture of birds is a sticky matter for cat and bird lovers alike. We praise and admire our feline mouse killers, but we tread on touchy ground when we talk about cats killing birds. The lovely songbirds seem so innocent, their demise so utterly tragic. It is crushing to find a dead bird on the back porch—I don't think anyone is arguing that point. Yet cats aren't cruel, they're only doing what cats do naturally. Bird hunting is etched into every feline fiber and regrettably nothing is going to dissuade them from chasing and nabbing our feathered friends.

There are however, a couple of tactics to minimize the success of your feline bird hunter. Cat collars fitted with a small bell work well to announce their presence to the local bird population as kitty prances around the backyard after them. Alas, some cats work to remove the annoying bell or learn to walk so stealthily that the bell does not sound. Ironically many of us who love and want to keep cats also love and want to attract songbirds. Unwittingly we further complicate matters by turning our backyards into songbird feeding stations. So what is a person to do? Try limiting the number of bird feeders around the property. Feed the birds where the cats cannot reach or access easily. Use every deterrent you can think of to protect the birds from your highly skilled cat and then, well, consider letting the natural animal world do its thing.

Remember that the drive to become an exceptional hunter and stay an exceptional hunter is pretty much what a cat is all about. It's what excites them and keeps them the happiest. If your cat is granted the delights of the outdoors, you might need to choose between feeding the birds and feeding your cat if your goal is zero bird kill. The two aren't always mutually exclusive but if you do feed the birds you'll be forced to accept the reality that you are going to lose some backyard birds. Even without bird feeders your cat is likely to catch a sweet bird. This is a tough problem to solve... there's not a great solution and it's a thorny, controversial issue to navigate. Good luck. You're going to need it.

WHY DO CATS BRING US THEIR LATEST CATCH?

Kitty wants to teach you how to hunt! The cat considers herself quite the skilled hunter and she considers you, well, quite the opposite. By delivering to you her latest prey, she's saying, "Hey, look what I've just caught! Wouldn't you like to learn how to hunt, too?" Your gracious response should be something like, "Oh thank you, what a good hunter you are" and "Yes, I'd like to learn, but this isn't a good time." Praise the cat profusely for her sincere efforts at apprenticeship training, wait until the cat is out of sight, and then dispose of your "gift" as quickly as you can. Seriously, cats do feel it is their responsibility to teach us humans about hunting, just as a mother cat methodically demonstrates to her kittens how to catch and eat a mouse. The process begins with mother cat bringing home a dead animal and progresses to Mama offering live prey to her kittens. Finally, the kittens join mother cat on the hunt and try it on their own. Since most adult cats are accustomed to watching their kittens participate earnestly in hunting lessons, don't be surprised if your cat looks puzzled and even disappointed when you are less than effusive about the whole thing.

WHY DO CATS OVEREAT?

I f she could, kitty would tell you not to read this section. Eating is a pleasurable activity and while the goal is good health, it's just plain comforting too. Most cats overeat because they are over-fed. While some cats self-feed from a continuous "bistro" type feeding system and effectively manage their own portion control, most cats do not know when enough is enough. Cats will also eat when bored. It is incumbent on the humans to look out for kitty's health and well-being when it comes to what, when and how much lands in the food bowl.

Cats require a high protein, lower carbohydrate diet of canned or dry cat food. The better quality cat foods are going to cost more—there's no getting around that. Consult a higher end pet supply store to learn more about reading cat food labels; you're going to need a translation of the exact ingredients in that bag you're holding. (Watch out for the local vet's recommendation: some vets are paid to promote and sell a certain brand of pet food and it's normally quite a popular product, but not necessarily superior.) Once you've chosen a nutritious cat food, follow the portion guidelines carefully. The extra calories in a heaping scoop of food day after day are going to add pounds. You'll feed according to age, weight and activity level.

If the directions on the package of food do not contain this type of feeding chart, you've got the wrong food. Make a plan and stick with it. Keep water bowls fresh and full at all times—water intake is absolutely essential.

Okay, so what about those tasty treats we love to give our cats? Upscale pet stores offer a tempting array of kitty treats and we can be made to feel like the dullest pet owner when we refuse to purchase them from the enthusiastic salespeople. These treats are packed with calories and it's easy to slip kitty this or that throughout the day without realizing she's consumed a meal's worth in snacks alone. One or two treats per day is a fine plan.

If you're feeding kitty the proper amount of food and she's gaining weight you've probably got a sedentary cat on your hands. Either decrease the daily caloric intake or increase the exercise or both. Even adult cats ought to be invited to play. Get creative, get moving, get those cat toys out and make life more interesting for the feline in your midst. Cats who are allowed outside to explore get much more exercise than their strictly indoor counterparts so you might want to consider those benefits.

WHY DO CATS LASH OUT?

Most of the time, a cat needs a darn good reason to lash out at the people in his or her life. Either the cat has fallen into a bad habit that might relate to the past, or it is reacting to something disagreeable in the present. An otherwise friendly cat with a good disposition that regularly scratches and bites the hand that feeds and pets him is distressed. It could be trauma or repeated mishandling from the past, or it could be a response to the current home situation. Rescued cats from tough conditions require time to be convinced that the person coming near is not about to mistreat them… and because you are the one who took on this cat, you might get a bit roughed up in the process. (Tip: this will seem unnatural and ill-advised but don't jerk your hand away when kitty bites or claws. Keep it motionless, quickly blow a puff of air in kitty's face and stare him down—you'll show him you're not afraid and that you're not going to fight. You're now in the stronger position and kitty should stop the intimidation sooner than later.)

Another cause of lashing out is that kitty is experiencing petting in some unpleasant way such as too hard, too long or too often. Cats crave our affection, but sometimes a little physical touch goes a very long way. Learn to read your cat's body language and watch for signals. Some cats prefer to be asked if it's a good time for demonstrative affection. Be sensitive and notice what works. Stay aware of how children are treating the cat, too. They mean well.

Then there's the cat that lashes out in a more playful, unaggressive manner towards its loving human. In this instance you've got a cat who might be stuck in kitten hood when "play fighting" with littermates was acceptable and even encouraged by mama cat. Somewhere along the line, it has become the ritual for greeting you or the beginning of play time or a plea for attention. As a young kitten it was probably sweet but now it's just infuriating. (Refer to the tip earlier in this section.)

I'm also very certain that cats size us up when we come near to offer a scratch behind the ears or some other bit of "quality kitty time" and if they think this could be merely a cursory bonding moment, beware. The cat may "fire a warning shot over the bow" as if to say, "I'm going to bite (or claw) you now, because I predict you won't stick around very long for this petting session and I'm not at all pleased about that."

WHY DO CATS LIKE PAPER BAGS?

To a cat, the basic brown paper grocery bag is a crisp, fresh new toy, just waiting to be personally scent-marked, cleverly hidden within, ripped and pounced upon. Kitty views this toy as something she can use for hunting practice, which is what feline playtime is all about anyway. Cats love to pretend that they are stalking prey and a stiff brown sack works quite well for this. They can hide behind or inside it, they can move it across the floor, and then enthusiastically pounce at the trapped imaginary critter. The bag holds its shape pretty well but also scrunches and smashes to further add interest to the hunting game. Cats like things that make interesting sounds and the crinkle of paper is one of their favorites. Stick a fake mouse inside the bag or tap the outside when the cat is crouching inside to mimic the patter of little creature feet, and you'll be providing kitty with some exercise and mental stimulation. Older bags usually lose their appeal after awhile so it's best to pull out a new one often. (Avoid using bags with handles as kitty can get tangled.)

WHY ARE CATS SO UNPREDICTABLE?

When it suits kitty, he loves to do things exactly the way they've always been done and in fact will insist upon it. But predictability is overrated and not always a plus, especially when you're talking cats. Dogs are more predictable than cats. With few exceptions, you know what a dog is going to do if you've done the training. The canine works diligently to behave according to your expectations. Not so with kitty. There's a wondrous dichotomy within the feline—an animal full of ritual and disciplined routines on the one hand and an untamed beast on the other with a rich, complex psyche. It's been this way for centuries upon centuries and it won't be changing anytime soon.

Sharing your space with a cat is a great deal like living with a wild animal—and wild animals are unpredictable. Ultra cat-people find this fascinating, but you may find it unsettling. For the sake of survival cats are unpredictable, sneaky and clever when on the hunt, and in the rare instances, when the cat is the hunted one. Surprise moves are coveted. Wherever the independent feline carves out an existence—in the jungle, savannah, pasture, city or suburbia, it is critical that its hunting skills are honed to a level that surpasses the neighbors' hunting skills. You get to witness bits of this undomesticated behavior nearly every day when kitty lurches, lunges, stalks, climbs, snarls, jumps and you might forget for a moment that you're not in the jungle. Coursing through the cat's body are ancient genes that propel them to act this way. They've also got a mighty fine reputation to uphold.

Not unlike an artist, the feline will approach an ordinary experience in a manner which it's never quite been done before. Watch for this and celebrate it. Its art in motion and kitty loves to keep you guessing. One moment your cat lies serenely curled in your lap and the next he is adamantly patrolling his territory with the seriousness of a military guard. Just when you've got him all conveniently figured out the show changes. Cats like it that way.

WHY DO CATS PURR?

Cats make the world a sweeter place just by exuding this yummy, audible vibration. Most purring, by far, is the cat's way of expressing utter contentment and joy, something like the deep, warm, sincere smile of a human. However, kitty may also use the alluring purr to get your attention, to smooth over a wrong, or to try and make you give in.

A cat may also purr when approaching another cat with whom it wants to play, not fight; it's a sign of friendliness when the cat community is out socializing. An extremely sick, defenseless cat may purr when a person or animal comes near in an effort to calm any aggression that might arise from this potential enemy. Female cats purr when they are in labor. Mother cats purr as they near their blind and deaf newborn kittens to reassure them that it's only mama cat coming near to nurse. The kittens purr back in response to signal that they are receiving their mother's milk. Scientists are not certain precisely where in the cat's body the purr originates or exactly how the body physiologically pulls it off. How fitting that the purr would be so elusive! What is known and widely accepted is that the purring sound is made from the rapid pulling apart of two vocal chords—some say "false" vocal chords because they are two membrane folds behind the actual vocal chords. Cats purr at the rate of 26 cycles per second, which explains why purring is likened to the sound of a whirring motor. The feline is the only animal in the world that purrs. Come now, are we really that surprised?

WHY DO CATS NEED THEIR CLAWS?

'm going to answer this question with another question: Why do we need the tips of our fingers? Ouch. While that comparison might seem ludicrous, it's a good analogy for what happens to a cat when it is subjected to the extensive surgery referred to as declawing. A more apt term would be "de-toeing" for that is closer to the truth. The claws of a cat are an impressive set of tools that first and foremost give kitty the edge in snatching prey. With one perfect swipe of those razor sharp claws in combination with their legendary feline precision and speed, that's one fantastic hunter. If cats are anything, they are hunters and the claws are essential. A cat also employs his claws as first defense against an enemy—whether actual foe or merely a threat. Many a cat has thwarted the aggression of a larger animal by displaying his claws at just the right moment. Sometimes the antagonist proceeds wisely and escapes unharmed and sometimes, well, he foolishly does not. Once a cat hooks his attacker with its claws, you don't want to stick around for the teeth.

Cats also need their claws for climbing trees, fences and any surface they wish to scale. Indoors or outdoors, cats routinely look for escape routes, and the quickest option is usually vertical. (By the way, those marvelous claws are perfectly curved for grabbing on the way up, but not much good coming down, thus the common cat-stuck-in-the-tree scenario.) As for physical conditioning, digging their claws into something with resistance is the only way to stretch and tone the muscles of the back and shoulders. Even a cat stripped of its claws will instinctively make the clawing action, but without the ability to actually grab, hold and really reef on something, those important muscles aren't strengthened.

Because the cat's claws are vital for hunting, protection, escape and fitness, the ramifications for the "declawed" feline are enormous and I think, colossally cruel. Not only do cats lose their primary, age-old means of safeguarding and survival, they actually lose a good portion of their toes—ligaments, tendons, bones and all. The medical term for the surgery is an "onychectomy" or more precisely, amputation of the last bone in the cats toe, clear to the joint. Removal of this portion of a cat's toes is not only excruciating during recovery, it results in chronic back pain and imbalance because cats are "digitigrade"(they walk on their toes) and the entire weight of the cat is designed to be supported and distributed by the toes. Cats need their toes and their claws. Without them, cats must remain strictly indoors and heaven help them if they ever slink outside for a stretch in the sun or some fresh air. It is not difficult to understand why in many countries of this world, feline onychectomy is illegal.

WHY DO CATS HIDE UNDER THE BED?

Because it's the most difficult place from which to extract her, of course! That familiar spot is dark, relatively quiet, out of the way and hard to reach. When kitty dives under the bed in the back room she is running from a real or imagined threat and the objective is to become virtually invisible. For some reason the cat feels it necessary to sequester herself someplace very safe and secure. Is the atmosphere boisterous or might there be someone who habitually plays rough with kitty? Perhaps a new person or new pet has joined the family and kitty is peeved. Given their masterful memory for details about incidents in life from way, way back the fleeing feline could be recalling something truly scary.

I once worked with a cat for two hours when cat sitting for a neighbor to coax this kitty out from under the bed. We eventually carved out a nice friendship, but it required endless patience and effort including lying on the floor eye to eye with the cat and chatting softly and calmly for a very long time. This cat was fine with people she knew, but petrified of strangers and mere acquaintances. Some cats are severely shy for no apparent reason and never feel comfortable around guests, repeatedly choosing to hide under the bed or some other small, remote place. Avoid giving up on a shy cat who runs away to hide; it would be unfortunate to quit too soon and miss the breakthrough. Of course whenever a cat's behavior patterns change drastically it's wise to check for any contributing medical issues.

Regardless of why a cat decides to withdraw into the far-flung caverns of the house, it is probably going to need steady verbal reminders that its presence is desired. Cats do crave our reassurance that they are indeed wonderful, that we love having them around and that we sincerely miss them if they steal away. When opposite airs are given off it's only a defensive cover-up... and they're hoping we don't buy into it.

WHY DO CATS GET STUCK IN TREES?

t occurs at least once in the life of most every cat: kitty climbs higher and higher up into a tree and before he knows it, he's gone much farther than he'd planned. Peering down through the branches, sheer panic sets in when he realizes that it would require a long, risky jump to reach the ground. Next, kitty tries to use his claws to ease him down, but becomes acutely aware that his amazing claws are suited for climbing up a tree, not down. Cat claws are specially curved for one-direction traction and only when the cat goes backwards down a tree will the claws hook into the bark and keep him from falling. The pitiful, helpless cries of the stranded feline can be heard throughout the neighborhood and it doesn't take long for someone to follow the painful wailing sounds right to the base of a tree. With gentle, patient coaxing by a caring person most cats will figure out that they must back down the tree, and they will eventually do just that until their happy paws hit firm ground. Of course, nobody says it's easy to stand by and listen to a terrified cat try to climb down out of a tree, so get out the ladder and rescue kitty if you must, knowing that he may not learn this tree navigating skill if you resort to the quick fix.

WHY DO CATS INSIST ON TOTAL RUN OF THE HOUSE?

Well, mostly it's because your home happens to be smack-dab in the middle of their territory. In fact it's the nucleus, the very heart of their inner kingdom. If your cat is indoor-outdoor you might be wondering: since kitty has claimed so much outdoor turf, why does she need access to every square foot of the inside? To your cat, it's *all* her territory, every bit… and she feels obliged to traverse this space more than once each day to feel completely secure and at peace. And a secure, peaceful feline is a better behaved feline. Ideally, there would be no interior doors in our homes if cats had their druthers. A closed door to a room the cat typically visits is similar to a breach of contract from the cat's perspective. Once kitty has entered a space and scent marked its game over. Now if you never, ever let a cat into a particular area/room in your house and you religiously keep that area inaccessible your cat won't realize what's behind that door or press the issue to get in and explore. (It should be noted that indoor cat doors are becoming more popular as they save time and hassle.)

The other major reason cats feel entitled to move freely about our homes is because they consider themselves to be an integral part of our families—whether we regard them this way or not! This is how cats view themselves and it is how they think you see them, so any form of barrier is confusing and frustrating. If your household is in constant shuffle and you're balancing a jam-packed schedule, you may miss kitty's subtle and not-so-subtle signs that she feels excluded. When the cat cannot enter a room she's been in before, the demanding meowing and frantic scratching of doors and door frames is likely to ensue.

Young kittens should be corralled into a room when they are learning about litter boxes, what to claw, what not to claw and how to co-exist with the other feline members of the household. Other occasions for temporary confinement include lengthy (or loud) home repairs and construction projects. Do not isolate kitty for disciplinary purposes—it does not work and it will backfire. I certainly don't advocate for cats to be allowed upon kitchen counters, food prep surfaces or eating areas, however I do recommend inviting your feline to sleep on your bed; kitty may not accept every night or for the whole night, but she will certainly appreciate the welcome. And you just might like it too.

WHY DO CATS SIT DOWN ON WHAT WE ARE READING?

There are a few humorous theories to explain this phenomenon and I love them all. The first purports that the cat insists on being right in the middle of things, lathered with our full attention in a precocious, whenever-I-please-thank-you-very-much sort of way. Once you've lived with a cat, this explanation is very easy to believe.

It could also be true, however, that kitty isn't as overly confident as she seems, and her desire to have top billing every night is actually a sin-cere quest for reassurance that she is as incredibly adored as she was last night. The longer I know cats, the more I think this is true in many instances.

A third explanation for this forward, in-your-face kind of presence is possibly the sweetest of all: perhaps kitty notices that you are oh so busy and takes it upon herself to give you a little break from your work. Hmmm, the more I think about that one, the more I think kitty is pulling our leg, but it sure makes a nice story.

WHY DO CATS DRINK FROM THE TOILET BOWL?

Alright, here we go. I'm going to venture into the toilet bowl discussion and bravely tackle this disgusting habit of a surprising number of cats out there. Cat owners tend not to admit that their cats would stoop to such a thing as actually drinking the toilet water and I cannot say that I blame them. (I don't even like typing it.) Such strange behavior begs the question, "WHY??" on the part of cat people everywhere. After all, this is the chic, meticulously clean feline we are talking about and one can only say, "there's got to be a very good explanation for such uncharacteristic behavior." Well, there are a few decent theories drifting around among the experts that might get us closer to some understanding.

Several cat behaviorist types purport that the water in a toilet is attractive to some cats because it is cold and (presumably) fairly clean. The toilet bowl water is not interesting to cats because it's unclean or because they are fond of the urine smell or taste, otherwise they'd be licking the rim after a male in the house left the seat up, right? And thankfully we don't see cats doing that. It's hard to wrap our heads around the assertion that cats can only find clean drinking water in our toilet bowls for goodness sake, but there may be more to it than just that. Apparently, many cats seek water sources that are moving, flowing or in this case, flushing. That explains why cats often hang around toilets if they are waiting for them to flush. And cats are known to patiently wait for something they want. This makes sense when you think about all the other places from which cats drink water such as faucets, draining bathtubs or showers, even curbsides after a rain and backyard ponds with waterfalls. Perhaps with this penchant for circulating water in mind, manufacturers of pet equipment have designed "fountain" drinking water systems for cats that apparently attract kitty and help solve the toilet bowl problem.

Still others suggest that cats enjoy the process of "finding" their food and water as they had to do every single day in the wild. And reminiscent of so much else within the feline, their ancient patterns have only partially been shed. I suppose that looking for water to drink in the toilet every day could be nostalgic for the cat and who would want to take that away. (Okay, I would.) But heck, if the toilet is sanitized often enough and you don't use chemical cleaners that are toxic to cats; I guess there's no cause to worry. You don't have to like this odd kitty quirk and of course if you cannot tolerate it for whatever reason, keep the darn lid down!

WHY DO CATS SIT AND STARE?

They do that for absolutely no reason at all… and for a thousand reasons. While we humans would doubtless feel self-conscious sitting and staring out the window or up at the ceiling for prolonged periods of time, the feline is unaffected. In fact, the practice has now turned into a fine skill. And it's relaxing to watch a cat watching something else… for surely they are looking at *something*, right? That frozen stare is hopefully not a vacant stare or kitty might be suffering from a whole host of other problems. We're going to assume that the cat is well adjusted, healthy and fairly typical in her daily feline activities.

So what is she doing? What does she notice that we don't? Of course now and then the cat is peering outside and you're able to see what she's viewing by sashaying over to the window yourself. At first you might peek into the light of day or dark of night and see nothing—but if you stick around, scan the entire scene and pretend you're a cat with extraordinary vision it may get interesting. That tiny bird across the way will come into view; you may notice a slowly moving bug or someone could be walking down the street blocks away. Not much escapes the resident cat and that's the way she likes it. This is boring stuff to us, but cats track, analyze and remain fascinated by all the mundane movement in their world. Potentially it's anything but mundane if kitty spots prey or an unwelcome intruder. Cats lost in contemplation might also be observing various light patterns dancing on the wall or ceiling. A mirror, vase or prism could be throwing reflections about the room just enough to entertain the cat.

How about the occasions when the cat truly gazes at nothing whatsoever? Is she daydreaming? Is she miserably bored? Why do we need to know? Are we envious? Is that a luxury we feel that we cannot afford? Maybe she's scheming or imagining or pretending. Whole books are written about what cats could be thinking at any given time and we do love to surmise and anthropomorphize. I'm guilty too, because it's amusing to guess and wonder what's going on in there.

WHY DO CATS SHIFT THEIR WHISKERS IN AND OUT?

Besides contributing to those famous feline good looks and perhaps reminding us of a mustache, the cat's whiskers are great mood indicators.

When a cat's whiskers are clumped together and pressed close to kitty's face, she is feeling extremely timid, shy or defensive. Conversely, when the whiskers are fanned out and spreading, the cat is tense for one reason or another—not necessarily nervous, but certainly excited. This whisker display doesn't automatically indicate that kitty will attack, but it is the one cats use just before an aggressive move. Depending upon the circumstances, she could become threatening, but more than likely she is simply being her benevolent inquisitive self.

Some cats might also extend their whiskers as an ardent request for stroking and attention. The most common state-of-the-whiskers is full extension, out sideways, not spreading too far. Kitty is letting the world know that she's relaxed, comfortable, friendly, content, ambivalent, or even bored.

The cat reserves the right to hold plenty of mystery—and to be honest, we probably wouldn't have it any other way.

WHY DO CATS GET FLEAS?

This is a trick question. Cats don't get fleas—fleas get cats. And fleas are seemingly everywhere… although in some regions or neighborhoods they are unusually thick. Farms are infested due to the presence of assorted farm animals and livestock. Some years are worse than others too. A misnomer about fleas is that you've got to have a pet to attract fleas; yet even homes without pets can be crawling with the blood sucking buggers if they hitch a ride on a pant leg or shoe. Fleas are like miniature heat seeking missiles that can detect a warm blooded animal from who knows how far away. Adult fleas can survive without a blood meal (ick!) for up to 14 days at which point they will die. Unfortunately, the same cannot be said for flea eggs and larvae which can remain in the indoor or outdoor environment for months without a 'host' or animal. This is why flea populations can mushroom rapidly and why they're so difficult to control.

Dealing with fleas is miserable and exasperating for all pets and people involved. You'll need to treat the cat and the environment to eliminate the fleas and prevent further outbreaks. The product you drop or ooze onto the back of the cat's neck every month or so is the easiest and most effective method of killing the fleas on the animal. You could still have fleas in the house though, and that's where you'll need a chemical dust to filter down into the carpet and upholstery fibers (where the fleas live when they're not sucking blood from your cat) and destroy all stages of the fleas including egg, larvae and pupa. Stay one step ahead by regularly treating your cats and your home before the situation gets out of hand. Use an odorless insect growth regulator for uncarpeted areas.

Vacuuming is a great way to remove the 'flea dirt' (dried blood/flea excrement) which the pupa and larvae use for sustenance to develop to the next stage. It also rids the house of various and sundry debris that the younger stages of fleas incorporate into the building of their cocoon or casing. Yes, you're waging all-out war against these insidious little pests and you're going to destroy their habitat and not feel badly about it! Pay special attention to areas the cat uses for sleep and play. And don't forget to treat and vacuum under the furniture; fleas do hide after all.

Outdoors, keep things raked and generally cleaned up. Tall weeds and other plants that have gone to seed attract and feed wild animals and that brings more fleas. Remedies for the outside areas include spreading granules and applying solutions that kill or repel fleas. Purge the existing fleas and prevent future residents with gusto and get ready for battle. To the death!

WHY DO CATS LIKE SMALL SPACES?

A cat can make quick work of disarraying even the tidiest linen closet or lingerie drawer. Cats are fond of closet shelves, drawers, baskets, boxes, and other hideaways because they feel snug and protected in smaller, defined places. The sides of a basket, the walls of a box (even a box lid) or a stack of pillows all provide a miniature fortress for kitty when she wants to slip away unnoticed or simply enjoy an undisturbed nap. (I think most of us can relate.)

A cat who is especially fearful or upset might be found under beds and sofas—the harder to reach, the better.

Kitty's love of cramped quarters is why cats don't mind cat carriers. From the cat's point of view, if the humans insist on hauling them to the dreaded vet and back, please let it be in a sturdy, secure carrying case. It is the unusual cat who prefers to roam the inside of a car and kitty usually ends up under the seat anyway.

WHY DO CATS DETEST BEING TEASED?

'm quite certain the word itself does not exist to the cat. From the cats' point of view, teasing is confusing and irritating at best. One glance at the expression on a cat's face and you can often read bewilderment, uneasiness or even blatant terror. By contrast dogs seem to live for teasing and it's a major part of their play with people. Only when cats are involved in hunting practice (their only reason to play) can one observe any kind of teasing but beware, there's a catch. The rule never to be broken is this: it's only the cat that does the teasing. Never, ever is kitty the one teased. When a cat is hunting for sport (rather than sheer hunger) it may mercilessly tease its prey and think nothing of it.

Anything that hints of teasing is eventually met with distrust and perhaps bitter revenge. Once things spiral out of control to that degree you're likely to have a nasty, spiteful cat to deal with… perhaps for the rest of its life. The cat's memory is superior and he does not forget sins committed against him. And in the world of the feline teasing is a cardinal sin. At all cost, steer clear of mocking, pestering, harassing, provoking, baiting, taunting or chasing the cat in your life. These things do not compute to kitty and will only instill fear. A cat may forgive if it thinks you ignorantly made the mistake, learned from that mistake and have sincerely reformed. However if kitty suspects you're tormenting her for the fun of it and your misdeeds are calculated, better watch out… your feline friendship is in jeopardy. Teasing is that big of a deal to a cat.

Watch cats at play to recognize what they think is enjoyable and entertaining and then join in the play. Cats love to bat at dangling things, flick small items across a floor, toss something lightweight into the air and chase flying or darting things. Your goal is civilized, tame and orderly play. Don't even think about pretending to chase the cat and whatever you do, don't growl or make fierce animal sounds. Save all of that riotous, frolicking nonsense for the canine in your life. Dogs cannot get enough teasing and regularly beg for a game of chase and who-is-tougher-than-who. It is baffling to the cat why this would ever occur unless it was real. At the very least it will strain the satisfying relationship you're building with your cat. You've probably got a great thing going… don't blow it now.

WHY ARE CATS MISUNDERSTOOD?

Over the course of their long and enduring existence domestic cats have tolerated countless misconceptions pertaining to all things feline. At one point in history cats were actually thought to be evil incarnate and their numbers diminished for many, many years. Centuries later we're still dealing with the vestiges of a genuine fear of cats, widely held cat myths and a lingering skepticism. Despite the bitter realities of rejection and gloomy isolation the stoic feline has shouldered it all quite well. Cartoonists haven't helped the cause by stereotyping cats as totally self-serving. Neither has the dark holiday at the end of October offered much help, presenting the cat in a most unapproachable light. In the last half century great strides have been made to smother the mythical cat tales and thankfully the feline is well on its way to redeeming himself.

One of the most common complaints from non-cat people is the perception that cats are aloof and stingy with affection. I believe that many cats who are aloof have become aloof because the people in their life are aloof, thinking the cat is aloof. Sometimes a cat's self-reliance is misconstrued to mean self-involved. Most cats are affectionate, but one might not be able to fully enjoy this if the cat is not shown affection first. With a need to be sure of your desire for affection they wait for you to make the first move. It may not be what we're used to hearing, but cats are sentimental after all and long to be invited to come close and stay close. A tender, persistent approach builds a cat's trust and once they see that this connection is the real thing and not a passing fancy, you will encounter a new kind of relationship.

Cats want to be loved and valued for just exactly who they are, nothing more and nothing less. Too often people make negative assumptions about cats based upon their familiarity with dogs. It's unfair to compare cats to dogs except for the purpose of contrast to better understand the feline (or the canine). For those willing to fling aside all erroneous beliefs about cats and diligently study the cat with humor, whimsy, respect and an open mind, the benefits are rewarding. It's like when kids leave the nest and then come back to visit; they're grown up, independent and not obligated to come around but they have clearly decided they want to. And that's golden.

WHY DO CATS BAT AT DANGLY THINGS?

Cats are acutely interested in any small thing that is fast moving or any small thing that they can easily get to move fast with a flick of their deft little paws. Why? Well for one thing, it's just plain fun, but most importantly, it is a highly-prized hunting skill that cats simply love to hone. What great pleasure and satisfaction kitty feels at the ability to adeptly snatch things with consistency and precision, especially objects that happen to be bobbing, dangling, or otherwise moving around erratically. Flying things are particularly tempting and remind kitty of winged insects, birds and even fish—and their vivid imagination doesn't need a whole lot to create a rather intense game. For a cat, the tougher the challenge of capture the better—it only boosts their confidence and swells their pride. Of course, being the cheeky characters that they are, cats may not always possess the most altruistic motives for batting at stuff; at times their main objective might be attracting your attention and they know that tugging at the floating fern frond or the swinging drapery tassel will guarantee plenty!

WHY DO CATS HATE LOUD NOISES?

The ears of a cat are sensitive to the faintest of sounds that our ears cannot begin to register. With their highly developed sense of hearing, a cat's ears rotate an astonishing 180 degrees to pick up reverberations like the tiny tamp of a mouse foot on an earthen floor or the slightest rustle in the grass, all from yards and yards away. Noises that are raucous to our ears are *really* loud to them. If the music is ear piercing to us, it's deafening to the cat. High pitched noise is uniquely aggravating to cats as their ears are engineered to detect the upper frequencies especially well. The sensation is often painful and most cats will head for the relative quiet and comfort of a favorite hiding spot.

Causing further anxiety for the cat is the fact that big noises come without any indication of what or who made the clang or clatter. Thunder is unnerving, huge and "out there" somewhere; does the cat wonder if it's a giant elephant that will come stomping into the room? Perhaps kitty never quite figures it out. Firecracker booms could be an air raid and the blaring power saw from the garage might be an alien. What's to prevent it from walking through the door any second? Even a loud jet overhead can be disquieting for the cat. Kitty not only thinks, "What the heck is that" but, "*where* the heck is that"… "and can I escape if I need to??" No wonder the cat vanishes to safety and does not emerge until the coast is clear.

It's critical (and kind) to provide a place of refuge for cats during noisy social gatherings, firework displays, construction work and the like. Note where the cat retreats and make sure kitty can reach it and stay there, undisturbed. An unusual, excessive fear of noises (loud or not so loud) can signal major insecurities within kitty stemming from past trauma or something in the current environment that's disconcerting. Cats from abusive situations may react dramatically to even minor noise and these animals require plenty of time and soothing reassurance to develop trust.

WHY DO CATS LIKE HIGH PLACES?

High elevations are attractive to kitty because they're relatively safe and because the view is ever so much better from several feet in the air! Whether it's overlooking the backyard or the living room, the feline must, must, must regularly monitor her territory—the higher the perch the better. Unless deep into sleep, the cat doesn't want to miss a thing. She logs all the comings and goings of housemates, her human companions, prey and potential enemy. Trees, fences, and rooftops outside the house and window sills, sofa backs, and entertainment centers inside the house are favorite watchtowers for cats.

Regardless, the whole idea is for kitty to check out absolutely everything from a secure site, high above danger. Of course no self-respecting cat would pass up the opportunity for a nice, peaceful elevated nap either. Who could blame them?

WHY ARE CATS ANNOYED BY DOGS?

One of the biggest reasons cats are annoyed by dogs is what we've covered in the previous section—the nearly unrelenting desire on the part of dogs to tease and be teased! There is apparently zero capacity within the sensitive, relatively serious-minded feline for comprehending the antics of the average dog, let alone a wish to be included. Cats look upon those frisky, romping dogs and try as they may, cannot fathom the inner workings of the canine mindset. And that's okay because the dogs are equally stumped about what makes cats tick. It's all a muddle that those of us with both cats and dogs get to referee all day long. Unfortunately the endless mixed signals and ensuing spats usually end up entertaining the good-natured dog while the poor cat simply endures.

What's funny is that dogs presume to know what cats are thinking and vice versa. The scenario unfolds like pages from a well-rehearsed script: Dog spots cat. Dog grins and barks excitedly in hopes that (boring) cat will be enticed into a lively game of chase. Cat is incensed that dog insists on assuming an aggressive posture (with cheerfulness no less) and hisses sharply in dog's face. Dog likes the sound effects and thinks, "Cool, I like how you've added hissing to add even more realism to your fear and anger!" Cat lowers ears. Dog thinks, "Love it! You're getting into it now. I'll bark and get down low like I want to attack you

and it will be awesome, dude." Cat either lunges at dog with claws extended or dashes away… at the very least perplexed and exasperated by the dog's concept of play and at worst, flat out terrified.

Watch a cat observe the larking about of a dog and their face says it all. The eyes are wide open in disbelief and they look from their human to the dog and back again as if to say, "Why is that animal so strange and juvenile? And furthermore, why do YOU compound the problem by acting strange and juvenile with him?" For all the smarts that both animals possess it's a head scratcher why neither one can figure out what the other one intends! Alas, there could be so much middle ground. If a kitten is raised with a dog and slowly learns by experience that a particular dog is kind and harmless, albeit a little nuts, a cat and dog can share a warm friendship.

If a cat is poetry perhaps a dog is a knockdown, drag 'em out action adventure story. If a cat is a romantic, artsy foreign film, a dog could be categorized more like a sturdy, faithful feel-good movie. Living with both a cat and dog is a great way to view their many disparities up close and completely celebrate them for their tremendous contributions to the animal world and of course to our own. So don't put your camera away too soon—you may find them curled up together yet.

WHY ARE CATS LAZY?

Maybe we can settle this once and for all—cats are not lazy. They do require more sleep and they know how to pace themselves. Much has been made of the cat's apparent idleness, but mostly by non-cat people who are more familiar with the ever-ready dog. Undeniably, the feline may seem slothful and some might actually be, but not intrinsically due to the fact that they are feline. If cats were lazy they would neglect their duties and their grooming and in these areas they are fastidious. If a typical day in the life of a cat is compared to a typical day in the life of a dog, the cat will certainly look like a slouch in contrast. But dogs are put together differently.

Physiologically, the feline body is suited for short bursts of intense energy and long interludes of rest which is ideal for—you guessed it hunting. Their state of alertness even while asleep is remarkable. Some experts believe that what a cat lacks in depth of sleep he compensates for in length of sleep. From long ago in their illustrious history the feline is fully prepared to sprint, leap, pounce and pierce with absolute precision at a moment's notice and that is not something a cat

takes lightly. He trains for it and conserves his strength for it. He is conditioned and smart about it. He's incredibly athletic and well-toned. Okay, at this point you might be chuckling as you think of your overweight blob of fur that rarely moves a muscle or lifts an eyelid as you pass by. With age cats do slow down and an overweight and under stimulated cat can surely become lethargic but that's ordinarily not the fault of kitty. And don't mistake boredom for laziness. Unless somebody decides to become kitty's helpful work-out partner to keep his brain active, his muscles conditioned and his lungs and heart in top shape he may succumb to an embarrassing state of couch potato sluggishness.

So just how much sleep does a cat need in a normal day? A healthy, active cat averages 16 hours of sleep per 24-hour period. And yes, you perceive this correctly—that is a ton of sleep and it's nearly twice as much as most other mammals need. It could be worse! If you kept a bat or an opossum for a pet you would seldom catch them awake as they sleep their lives away by snoozing a whopping 20 hours a day.

WHY DO CATS DASH MADLY AROUND THE HOUSE?

Relax, they don't do this to drive you crazy. Flying around at speeds of up to 30 miles per hour, cats who tear around the house with no apparent stimuli are merely burning off vast quantities of stored energy. This is perfectly normal feline behavior, especially for a mostly indoor cat who doesn't get enough exercise. Being nocturnal animals, the house will usually turn into a racetrack at night when cats would naturally hunt.

In the wild, cats sleep by day to store up the energy to chase and kill by night. For house cats, a meal is hand delivered and it is not incumbent upon kitty to fetch for himself. The instinct to run and chase and catch prey is still very much alive and well, however.

So if you're awakened by your cat's late-night antics, try to remember that this is an indication that kitty is actually quite sane and healthy, albeit a little under exercised. Roll over, go back to sleep, wait until the light of day… and tomorrow you can learn to play indoor soccer with your cat.

WHY DO CATS RUN WHEN THEY SEE A LEASH?

For the vast majority of the cat population a leash is an anathema. The feline detests being restrained, forced, tugged, pulled, pushed or otherwise coerced into doing absolutely anything. So the idea of being led around on a lead is unthinkable. The only way a cat would look upon the wrong end of a leash in any kind of remotely positive manner would be the realization that when on that leash (and only on that leash) he gets to go outside and explore. If you start leash training very young and before the cat experiences the out of doors by any other means, you might have a shot at success and a positive and gratifying experience for your feline. However, if you choose to defy the laws of probability and decide to introduce the leash to your adult cat who has already tasted outdoor freedom, it's probably going to be most unpleasant. Your dear cat will surely think you've lost your mind. Remember, this walking-tied-to-the-end-of-something goes against the grain of all things feline so don't expect rapid progression.

Do not think "dog" on a walk with a cat. It's usually not much of a walk at all but more like a "stop and go" excursion with the emphasis on stopping. You may not cover much ground at all. People will stare or do a double take. Always remember that you are giving your otherwise-relegated-to-the-indoors cat with a chance to be outside. Praise kitty generously. Eventually kitty will probably see the leash and get excited, even scoot to the door in anticipation of the adventure outside those walls. A harness might be a good idea if the cat is wiggly or easily spooked; some cats will tolerate a harness, some won't.

There are a couple of potential hazards to watch for on your stroll with the cat. Be alert to dogs that would cross the cat's path and throw him into a tizzy—that could send you backwards in your quest to leash train. Also, watch for trees that a cat might scamper up before you realize what has happened and then you have two problems… a cat stuck in a tree and a cat in danger of hanging itself on the leash if he should panic and attempt to jump down. Walking cats after dark seems to be the preferred time of day for an outing as their nocturnal programming puts them into a more confident and relaxed frame of mind. And you definitely want that.

WHY DO CATS SPEND SO MUCH TIME LICKING AND GROOMING THEMSELVES?

Cats devote nearly a third of their day to careful grooming, so I think we can safely say they are obsessed! Sometimes it indeed seems like overkill and we wonder just how dirty is this cat?

Of course, what kitty isn't telling you is that there are several perfectly good reasons for her fastidiousness besides a penchant for keeping clean. The earnest licking not only cleans and deodorizes kitty's coat, but also removes loose hair and skin, increases her blood flow, and tones her muscles. Think of it as part of kitty's daily workout routine.

Some cats also groom themselves when they are uncertain how to behave in a certain social situation or when they are unusually nervous—merely sitting there looking awkward would never do for a dignified feline!

Cats may also lick their coats to regulate body temperature. In the cold, repeated licking smoothes down the fur and acts as an insulating layer. On hot days, kitty may lick her fur to feel the cooling effects of evaporation, much as we benefit from the evaporation of sweat on our skin. And when it's raining, there's some automatic waterproofing going on—the licking stimulates glands in the skin that secrete a natural protective substance.

WHY DO CATS LOVE TO BE GROOMED?

Nearly all cats seem consumed with grooming. And while appearance does matter a great deal to the feline, I don't think it's all vanity. Cats are highly conscious of their coats and devote hours each day to keeping that glorious fur clean and sleek. It's about hygiene, health and well-being. Since cats groom themselves frequently, if not obsessively, perhaps we don't realize their need and desire for human participation.

When we pick up a cat brush or flea comb and stroke kitty, we're assisting with the removal of all sorts of debris, mites and those intrepid fleas. (Finding "flea dirt" on the flea comb is often the first sign your cat is playing host to the darn things.) Brushing the cat's fur keeps it glossy and rids the coat of loose hairs that would be swallowed by kitty and cause the dreaded hairballs. A cat's coat naturally thickens in fall and sheds in spring, but many cats now live in controlled climate environments (heat and air conditioning) and they are nearly always shedding. More shedding equals more ingested hair and a build up inside the stomach and intestinal tract. Long haired cats with silken tresses require almost daily brushing but short haired cats need plenty of brushing too. Long haired cats need extra help to prevent painful mats that are miserable for kitty to live with and painstaking to remove. A vigorous, but not too robust, brushing also helps blood circulation which promotes good general health. But it doesn't stop there. Staying hands-on provides a nice opportunity to check the cat for skin problems, infection, lumps or other serious conditions that might otherwise remain undiscovered until the next veterinary appointment.

Whether a cat cleans himself or we get involved in grooming, the experience is relaxing and stress relieving for kitty. Grooming is also great bonding for you and your feline. Incorporate brushing and even massage into a comforting routine which the cat looks forward to immensely at certain times of the day. Does it start her day or end it? Does it happen at the computer? Perhaps the grooming ritual occurs on your lap during morning coffee? If you watch a cat groom itself, you might notice a pattern. Cats lick their coats at the end of naps and after eating. They usually clean themselves in the same sequence every time so as not to miss a speck.

A word about cats that are overweight: an obese cat cannot reach its entire coat and must have grooming help from us. Most definitely implement a reducing plan, but in the meantime assist your cat and it will be grateful. Older cats will gradually groom less and less, but it's ever so kind to lend a hand and support them into old age.

WHY DO CATS DREAD BEING BOARDED?

The most effective way I can explain this is to attempt to climb inside the cat's mind and do a play-by-play from the feline perspective. Anyone care to join me? I'll state up front that I do realize there are circumstances in which all other cat care options have been exhausted and you simply must board the cat. I've done it myself in a royal pinch—that's one reason I've got some insight.

"Yo, dude. I guess I'm supposed to enlighten you about what it's really like to be sent to a 'cat resort' while you're gone on a trip. Oh wait, let's be honest here and stop referring to these places as cat resorts, kitty condos or cat town homes. You have got to be kidding. These places are prison. To begin with, we're kidnapped from our palace and surrounding kingdom only to be thrown into a cell that would be like relegating you to your walk-in closet. We don't have a clue where you have taken us or why. The dizzying array of *other* cat smells is driving us insane and we have no confidence whatsoever that you will ever return to retrieve us. We hate, hate, hate these places and we are stressed beyond belief that our territory back home has been left unguarded and vulnerable to attack or complete overthrow. You thought that adding cat TV and classical music would help? That's all stuff to distract us from the misery. And the token window? What's that about? To look out upon this inaccessible landscape that we can't explore and scent mark? How close am I to home anyway?

One chance and I'll disappear and go find it. At least make sure it's a cats-only facility... the dog whining, barking and general pandemonium that follows dogs everywhere might put us over the edge.

Dogs don't mind boarding and some love it because they are super social animals!! It's like summer camp—who will be there this year? What new tricks did they learn? Remember the old Frisbee I found two summers ago? I hope we get the same cabin, etc. We cats are busy staring each other down, noting who was placed where and why... anxiously wondering whose turf this is and how do we navigate through it? These people think it's so very clever to call this place a kitty vacation house? Oh the torment. I might be sick. People, this ain't no condo that I've ever been inside and it sure ain't a vacation. This is WORK. While you're sittin' by the pool on some island I'm at my wits end trying to figure out the rules and when my sentence is up. This is no picnic. You drop us off and say, have a nice rest? I'll be lucky if I sleep at all. If I ever get out of here... there might have to be some payback. This is ludicrous. I am a CAT. How could you not know I would despise this? Did you try all your cat sitter contacts? Did someone decide that if canines liked boarding, felines would too? Who conducted that research? You guys have got a lot to learn. Oh and speaking of learning stuff, I happen to know of this book..."

WHY DO CATS GET HAIRBALLS?

Also known as "furballs," cats develop these nasty knots of swallowed fur because of their need to groom incessantly, thoroughly licking their entire furry coats with their rough, scrub brush tongues. You've seen those sausage-shaped masses on the floor or carpet and you've probably heard the painful sounds coming from a cat attempting to spit one up. It is a dreadful event, but the cat feels great relief when the hairball is finally torpedoed out of there. Small amounts of hair usually pass through the cat's system easily; but not infrequently hair builds up inside, tangles, and forms a hard, matted clump that just doesn't budge. At this point, the cat must vomit up the hairball to keep it from blocking the digestive tract, which is a potentially serious condition. (Note: tubes of "hairball remedy" are widely available in stores and their weekly use is strongly encouraged to prevent and treat hairballs.)

Cats lose bits of hair all year long, but shed heavily in the spring and fall, so then there is even more loose hair around to become ingested. Long-haired cats battle hairballs more so than the shorthairs; however, a shorthair who grooms a longhair is at greater risk too. Seems like such a grim price to pay for staying clean!

WHY DO CATS SEEK OUT THE NON CAT PERSON IN THE ROOM?

t's uncanny how this works. Picture a room full of cat lovers waving at the cat or wooing him with assorted greetings, chirps or meows, only to observe the cat walk straight over to the people who are ignoring him. Cats love to do this and there are several opinions about why. Once thought to be further proof that the feline was a conceited, ill-mannered animal who took pleasure in pestering the classic "non cat person" at social gatherings, there is now conjecture that suggests the opposite. All the theories have merit and none contradict the others.

Perhaps the most charming notion is that cats enjoy the challenge of the guest who has not yet discovered the joy and adventure of friendship with a feline. The person uninitiated in the ways of the cat is a grand experiment, a mission to tackle, a situation waiting to be conquered. Kitty sniffs out the non-cat person and winds through their legs, sits at their feet and might jump onto their lap in hopes that, eventually, this cat-challenged human will slide on over to the cat lovers camp. It's crazy how often this strategy works! Some of these proud folk keep their newfound appreciation for cats a great secret for a long while… especially if they are known to be staunch cat avoiders. There's nothing quite like the satisfaction of witnessing a person who merely tolerates cats become a person who cannot imagine living without one.

Cats might also be attracted to the laid back attitude the self-proclaimed non-cat person exudes. Cat lovers can be overwhelming and effusive when a cat enters the room and sometimes kitty would rather head for a less fussy person. This type leaves the cat alone and has no agenda for a sappy short-term friendship at a party where cute quips and insincere smiles abound. Kitty appreciates how the non-cat person passively lets him establish his own contact at his own pace. But there's a hint of dysfunction here too. The cat could choose to hang with someone who genuinely likes him, but instead picks the person who would never be able to fully commit to an honest future relationship.

It's also been suggested that cats approach non-cat people who merely sit there with nary a look in the cat's direction precisely because they are unapproachable. This appears to make no sense, but the premise is that this kind of person is completely non-threatening and a cat would rather sit next to a dull stranger than an unknown spirited figure who is potentially dangerous. No, they are not going to be chums, but they aren't going to get into an altercation either. And sometimes the cat just likes to play it that way.

WHY DO CATS HISS?

They are mimicking snakes! It's true—cats and most other animals are dreadfully afraid of snakes and cats have chosen to imitate the deadly snake in order to terrorize another cat, a dog, other enemy, or even a person who appears hostile. A cat begins by flattening its ears and widening its jaw, thus taking on a snake-like appearance. You might see the tail swooshing back and forth too, which further suggests the movements of a snake. The actual hissing occurs when the cat opens her mouth part way, pulls back her upper lip, and forcefully releases her breath. Sometimes moisture accompanies the paralyzing hissing sound and then you get what is known as spitting. To be sure, hissing is an effective warning from kitty that seems to communicate in no uncertain terms that she is a force to be reckoned with. (Please note: be careful not to mimic the hiss in an attempt to stop your cat from doing something; you will cause her to be afraid of you and then you will become an enemy in her eyes instead of an ally or friend.)

WHY DO CATS END UP IN ANIMAL SHELTERS?

There are dozens of reasons why cats land in the local animal shelter. Many cats are old, troubled, abandoned or abused. A few are young and healthy (they get adopted first) and the majority are middle aged, moderately healthy stray cats, orphaned from the start. Rarely could a cat advocate visit a shelter and not depart without adoption papers firmly in hand. Peering through the cages are too many yearning, hopeful eyes and not nearly enough space in the homes of cat lovers to take them all. Strays make up the bulk of the cat shelter population. Neglected from the get go, these homeless cats are almost certainly not neutered or spayed, before being allowed to roam the streets and they are no doubt responsible for several litters before winding up at the shelter. On goes the ill-fated cycle. Legitimately lost cats are nabbed by animal control and brought to the shelter. If the owner seeks and finds the wandering cat all are thrilled with a happy reunion. If not, the drifter joins the cast and waits his turn for a chance at a stable, loving family.

Voluntary relinquishment is what happens when a person decides to rehome a cat that's been living with them. Motives for giving up one's cat vary from aggression to pet allergy. The cases in which the cat is aggressive to the point of being a real threat to people are relatively few. However, not all folks learn to work with their mildly misbehaving cat. Perhaps they shouldn't have agreed to a cat in the first place. Maybe they thought they knew cats, had a romantic idea of how life with a cat would be and now they're disenchanted. There's often not enough preparation before a pet is welcomed into the family. Studying cat care and behavior in advance of driving to look at any cat is critical. You're a goner if you meet an available cat and start to connect. Look online to view photos and see what strikes your fancy. If you like what you see, start reading everything you can get your hands on about cats.

Regardless, always specify a "no kill" shelter; perhaps one day all shelters will be "no kill." That's a day I'll look forward to. These incredible, hard-working rescue shelters are usually full to capacity with cats, as they only have space when there's an adoption, not because it's euthanize day like the place on the other side of town. Luckily cat foster homes are becoming more popular and I'd like to personally thank those folks from the bottom of my heart.

WHY DO CATS ROTATE THEIR EARS?

Because they can. If we could manage to turn, lower, and flatten our ears I suppose we'd show them off, too. But we cannot and they can, so cats use their soft, stylish, symmetrical ears to speak nonverbally to us and to other cats. Not only do their ears house intricate canals and receptors that grant the cat truly amazing hearing, they're also able to tell us much about a cat's state of mind.

When a cat's ears are tall and pointed forward, but slightly outward, kitty is content, aware, listening, and relaxed. Hopefully, this is how your cat looks most of the time. The ears could be facing different directions, depending upon where multiple sounds are coming from. (Try that yourself!)

When kitty's ears are facing straight ahead and totally erect, he's alert and focusing on a new sound; the cat is on guard and inclined to go investigate rather than curl up and relax.

Flattened ears mean the cat is frightened. Cats do this with each other when they are involved in a standoff; when the ears go down like this, it means something is about to happen. The cat could be seconds away from an all-out attack, or frightened enough to look for an escape route and run. Either way, kitty is pulling her ears down to protect them from being bitten and torn during a fight.

When the cat rotates her ears towards the back and then lowers them, she is very definitely angry and probably not frightened enough to retreat (or ears would be flattened). She is very likely to attack. You might notice these ears if your cat is ready to pounce upon another cat who has pushed too far. Hopefully, no one in your household will ever be the target of such behavior. (If so, it could mean that the cat has been mistreated.)

WHY DO CATS SLEEP ALL DAY?

They don't! Well all right, they do clock around sixteen hours of sleep during every 24 hour period and they are a nocturnal animal, but it would be a stretch to say that cats sleep all day long. (Some cats sleep out of boredom, but that's the owner's fault, not kitty's.)

You've heard the term cat nap? Well, it didn't originate from us. The cat's sleep patterns hearken back to its ancestors' life on the savanna when not a single hunting opportunity could be missed. A cat quickly and skillfully stalks and kills its prey, and thus must be ready to respond to a fast-moving dinner morsel at any given moment. The feline body is suited for short, potent bursts of energy and has adapted a sleep style to accommodate. Cats usually sleep lightly and more often, in order to gain in length of sleep what they may lack in depth. The cat is far from lazy, but instead has truly perfected the nap and mastered the art of pacing oneself throughout the day.

So the next time you pass by kitty all cozy and curled up, just remember that you are witnessing some highly efficient sleep management.

WHY DO CATS RUB AGAINST EVERYTHING IN SIGHT?

At the core of the answer to this question lies one of the most appealing characteristics of the feline. When a cat rubs against the corner of a sofa, the arm of a chair, a shoe in the hallway, or especially some part of a person, it is purposefully choosing the thing as its own. "This is mine more than it is yours," the ultra-territorial cat is announcing, and don't you forget it.

Whether cats are outdoors marking trees, steps, fences and benches, or indoors claiming furniture, walls, and people, they are very intentionally depositing their individual feline scent by way of special glands on the forehead, around the mouth, under the chin, near the ears, and even between the toes.

One rub is hardly enough though, as cats must continually refresh each spot they have visited to declare their rights to the next cat who comes along. Depending upon how many other cats step into his territory, a site might be frequented and marked several times per day.

When your cat comes alongside and tenderly nudges you, he's not only unabashedly declaring to the world that he considers you his property, he is also showing you genuine affection and a sincere desire for physical contact. As the cat lovingly slides its tail or chin along your leg, arm, or face with perhaps a slight pause and a purr, the unique scent he leaves behind is mingled with your unique scent (both undetected by our noses) which then produces a new "twosome" scent, something the cat finds great pleasure in creating over and over again.

Daily, incessantly, sometimes even forcefully and maybe not so quietly, the cat bonds with us, aligns with us, and attaches himself to us.

WHY DO CATS REFUSE TO COOPERATE?

The short answer is that cats are more like humans and less like dogs. We are accustomed to the joy that a dog exhibits when his master calls and he comes, or when he's told to sit and he sits, or when he faithfully returns with the Frisbee, and so on. Sure, dogs need some training and ongoing positive reinforcement, but by and large, the canine is a pack animal who is hardwired to accept and genuinely like following orders.

Not so the cat! The independent feline enjoys following orders about as much as we do. Cats will cooperate with people and other cats, but there has definitely got to be something in it for them.

Kitty is perfectly willing to arrive at your side when called, or hop down from that sensational napping spot when you ask him to, if he believes that something worthwhile will present itself when he does. The obvious rewards are tuna, milk, other special food treats, catnip, or a favorite toy or game. Less obvious rewards are things you do with and for the cat such as attentively petting him, greeting him warmly, or inviting him onto your lap.

Cats usually won't lift a paw to cooperate for cooperation's sake... but you'd be surprised what they'll do in the name of friendship.

WHY DO CATS' TAILS WHOP, WAVE AND QUIVER?

The tail of a cat is beautiful and graceful, all the while silently conveying much of what a cat would say if it could speak in words. It curls and dips and swooshes. It whips and darts and sweeps. A cat's tail floats through the air behind him as he walks and wraps right around him like a scarf as he sits. Besides its role as a kitty barometer, the feline tail is also used for balance (especially along a ledge or fence). Decoding every tail message isn't always possible, but there are a few tail positions we understand. A high flying tail is a good sign and usually means kitty is happy and secure in her surroundings. A tall quivering tail (from the base on up) is a sign that kitty is bursting with excitement or anticipation; a treat is about to land in her food bowl perhaps, or you have just walked through the doorway after being away. A whopping tail is either a sign of growing discontent (which may lead to anger), or a kind of excited indecision. For instance, kitty might be lying somewhere looking comfortable and even enjoying a good petting session when all of a sudden her tail will start whopping up and down or back and forth. She could be getting annoyed with the petting, or sensing that you're about to stop petting her. She may be deciding what to do next and has too many options. Cats also whop their tails when they notice prey, but do not (or can not) go after it. Vigorous whopping back and forth of the tail indicates that the cat is becoming quite irritated; her tail display could be warning of an attack. Most of the time, however, a whopping tail signals only moderate displeasure.

When the cat's tail slowly and very gently waves back and forth, she's happy, relaxed and delighted with what's going on. You might be stroking her, conversing lovingly, about to present her with a treat or even playing gently. She could be responding to a meaningful massage, the perfect scratch of her ears, or a great chin rub. Often the whole length of tail waves, but kitty could also curl just the tip of her tail to speak pleasure. Sometimes a cat's tail will whop and wave simultaneously, indicating her feelings at the moment are quite complex. She's loving some things and not so sure about others—now doesn't that just about sum up the cat?

WHY DO CATS "KNEAD" PEOPLE WITH THEIR PAWS?

Kneading is the very distinct trampling most cats do with their paws on the laps of their favorite people and upon soft surfaces around the house. The gentle pummeling action is used to deposit the cat's personal scent all around its territory, but what's really driving kitty to engage in this activity is pure pleasure.

Kneading, or "milk treading" as it's often referred to, is an endearing leftover from kittenhood when all the kittens would stimulate mama cat's milk flow by kneading her underside. For a kitten, these warm, snuggly moments with mama cat are total bliss and your adult cat still finds deep comfort in mimicking and possibly remembering its early nurturing. If your cat treads upon your lap often, it probably means she views you as a surrogate mother—especially if you are very quiet and relaxed, just how a mother cat would be during nursing.

You may be wondering about sharp claws digging into your skin during kneading and how you can enjoy this cozy bonding time as much as kitty! You might try only letting kitty knead when you're in thicker clothing or when you've got a blanket or throw to protect your legs.

Some cat experts discourage kneading as if the behavior fosters some immaturity in our cats, but cats really seem to love it and crave the warmth and security, so I join with many others and heartily say, why not?

WHY DO CATS BITE YOUR HAND DURING PETTING?

How dare she bite the hand that pets her! In her defense, your darling devil is most likely just showing good boundaries. While cats crave our undivided attention and love to be fussed over, they most definitely want it on their own terms. Unlike a dog—who never seems to get enough petting—a cat has firm, albeit fluctuating parameters for how often and how long she'll tolerate petting. Sometimes a few strokes will satisfy kitty's need for touch and at other times only a lengthy session of caresses will suffice. (Humans are actually not so different!) You'd have to be a mind reader to figure this out every time and perfectly accommodate kitty's delicate feline petting preferences, so now and then she makes it "easy" for you and nips at your hand when she's had enough. Or quite the opposite, some cats will take a preemptive bite as if to say, "I do hope these are not merely token strokes, and that you're not going to rush off before I've had my share." Like I said, cats know exactly how much petting they'd like and how often. They also reserve the right to change their minds several times per day.

WHY DO CATS COMPLETELY ENDEAR THEMSELVES TO US?

Now this is a mystery, for cats are so very capable of living life solo. They don't really need us, yet they like us, really. They desire our companionship—they want to be a member of the family.

They aren't known for making many promises, but they surely aren't the self-centered creatures they are often made out to be, either. Cats could so easily run away and have a perfectly interesting and satisfying life far away from humans, and in some ways it might be more efficient or feline-friendly: no loud music coming through speakers, no commotion during the day when they are trying to sleep, no wondering whether or not the food will truly arrive in the bowl.

Without us, there would be no limit of things to scale or climb, no breakables to dodge, no silly rules or strange customs. Yes, we do provide goodies and warmth and our cats know they've got it good, but it's far more than that. Don't underestimate the cat's capacity for love! The cat chooses friendship with humans and grants us entrance into their world—and in the process we become mesmerized by them.

We find that we will do almost anything for these creatures because they have become our friends and also because they are beautiful… and we enjoy this living, pulsating work of art right in our midst. The show is ever-changing, yet comfortingly the same. We are so lucky that this soft, silky, independent piece of wildness steps daily into our homes and announces through ears, tail, eyes, purrs, meows, body, and all else feline, that he is utterly content and that he wouldn't have life any other way. Well, that is, until tomorrow morning at 6 a.m. And you've just got to love that, too.